T BANDITS

The High Rollers

Alfonso Borello

T Bandits: The High Rollers Copyright © 2019 by Alfonso Borello. All Rights Reserved.

All rights reserved. No part of this book may be reproduced in any form or by any electronic or mechanical means including information storage and retrieval systems, without permission in writing from the author. The only exception is by a reviewer, who may quote short excerpts in a review.

Cover designed by Alfonso Borello

This book is a work of fiction. Names, characters, places, and incidents either are products of the author's imagination or are used fictitiously. Any resemblance to actual persons, living or dead, events, or locales is entirely coincidental.

Alfonso Borello
Visit my website at www.AlfonsoBorello.blogspot.com

Printed in the United States of America

First Printing: Aug 2019
Villaggio Publishing Ltd

CONTENTS

Chapter 1 1
Chapter 2 9
Chapter 3 15
Chapter 4 18
Chapter 5 24
Chapter 6 28
Chapter 7 33
Chapter 8 38
Chapter 9 42
Chapter 10 48
Chapter 11 52
Chapter 12 57
Chapter 13 63
Sci-Fi 68

Portions of this book appeared in the book **Giallo** by the same author Alfonso Borello.

T BANDITS

Chapter 1

"Tell Mom and Dad to write checks and put them on someone's insurance account, and I'll throw some fancy new bows on top of it, just for good measure."

Dr. Glasser stared at the write up on the chat room. Normally a calm person, lately his temper gets the better of him and makes him a target. Angry? Perhaps. RAGE YARD.

Inside the offices of the Federal Reserve, data scientists were busy researching the identity of the hacker responsible for the recent surge in Bitcoin trading volume. Before jumping on the micro-blogging service, he used the local coffee shop to get his messages across. As soon as the new posting was spotted by the eye and memory of the human eyeball, it began to spike the Bitkomato charts like crazy.

Carlos Christoforou, 27, a top IT engineer from Frankfurt, Germany, will pay the ultimate price for his incredible financial insight. Utilizing patient AI to monitor the markets, he was able to identify the underpinnings of the impending Euro crisis as early as September 2012, and unleash the full force of the

Alfonso Borello

regulatory kick before it could even hit the fan. There's just one catch: Frankfurt wasn't the only international financial center targeted by their devastating machine. More than one currency was trading with each hand; international banks like JPMorgan and Citibank were giving worthless USD banknotes a shot, while Spanish and Portuguese banks were racing to turn tricks the Americans left in the lurch.

Carlos needed only two swipes of the wrist, and the Euro was liquidated in his hand. The snow was falling badly. Chill. Cold.

Inside the offices of the Greek Finance Ministry, an elderly man dressed in black was smoking a cigarette. Two reporters crowded in a Johns Hopkins fugazi, and a university professor moved his finger. The ceremonial incused, white robes of the Greek Ministry of Finance fell to the floor.

A middle-aged Chinese-Dutch banker entered the room with the urn and started reading the Greek charter, which included provisions for a 1.5% annual bearish rate. The gracious wrinkled old face of the room sat down on the hardwood and made channels on a giant Chinese mobile phone.

The hall smelled institutional, so much the better. Redefining "institutional" equals swamp.

The clock on the air Conditioning unit read 4:20 ET. New York saw the post-crisis warning lights and—gasp—red rose by the Kremlin, while London realized history was on their side and Boris Johnson was king.

Time is 10:02 local. Berlin Hilton—hard to beat, nobody beats the market cap of the guy from Credit Suisse, period. Ajahn Chai Holy Shit!

T BANDITS

Rich kids getting richer. Shivers run down my spine. Getting sucked into the ever-changing ether isn't so bad, I swear. Hotels, fast cars, airlines, everything Swiss know how to play the market. Shanghai now joins the club with Champagne induced skin rash, no doubt. Skyscrapers burning to the ground.

"All right guys, it's moving! Market open end, high yield coin, stick with it and you could be the ninetieth trading club to collapse in on itself." Magic Johnson screaming and waving his fist.

Cameras flashed. Senators and representatives milling about. Cooler heads prevailed. No more low hanging fruit. Ben Cohen checking his mobile. Gravy can wait. Azteca back in vogue.

"Akk?"

His phone buzzed. He un-skimmed his Grease monkey, and shook his head, sipping on a Habanero hot beverage. His girlfriend, Emilia, pulled out a paper napkin and slapped on the paper, for the record.

"What's up?"
"Talk to you in a sec."
"Yeah, I made some new friends."
"How did they get my number?"
"Simone, the competition director from Angel List?"
"The trading coordinator from Kaistar?"
"Yeah, he told me about the trading."
"Let's get to work."
"Wait a minute."
"What?"
"Look at the CNY chart!"
Her eyes lit up. "Do we have any more money?"
"Nope. It was all taken out yesterday."
"All right guys, it's fucking hot in there damn it!"

"You should come out to the room, chill with the guys, and make some calls."

The apartment was already full of people, including a media celebrity from ESPN.com, who hung around on the second floor.

"You've been asking stupid questions."

"I have."

She glared at him; her smile was tinged with indignation.

He ignored her; he wanted to know what was going on.

"Have you guys had a chat yet?"

Ben shook his head, and finally adjusted his tie; it fits better in the vast ocean, rather than the closet it was originally hanging from.

"I haven't." Her eyes narrowed.

"We're just hanging out; she wants to meet someone."

A small startup guy from insurance mainlander AB Nation introduced himself.

Petticoat entangled in gnarled greasy brown hair, a smirk on his face. She stared at him; according to the pantomimic merchant, brand new set of MACs, Swiss bank account at HSBC, tax-exempt.

Hong Kong's International Financial Zone operator ICICI Bank is building a fancy new branch in Southeast Asia — and it's breaking new ground. Dedicated to trade finance, non-bond market orders, and foreign exchange trading, this branch will handle foreign exchange transfers at all-time low rates. Turkey is reportedly watching the joint venture fondly; one Western media source reports that senior bankers in Frankfurt and New York are super excited. My hotel was updated with a Jin

Jia news splash; Jiang Zemin, with eleven failed ICOs, is on the run for wire fraud, according to the chat rooms.

Bulgaria may decide to ratchet up the economic pain, or at least fortify its financial might. In the meantime, pleasantries for all.

Add another financier and good old China will look awfully familiar.

Did I read the fine print?

If I hadn't, I probably would have left a blank space.

After making more than a billion in a single day with his new craze, Johnson decided to settle for throwing another gong with his fellow Victorians.

It makes you wonder what the contract was on that one, Swiss account closed, 10,000 SEK penalty suspended, revenue 200,000 bases, balance limit 749,984,984%, Promissory notes converted to floating, trade at your own risk.

"Looks like comedy gold," wrote the bot on the computer at the front desk.

"I logged on to check the balance, and it's 10,030,354.40," I typed.

"You are now Houston/Chicagoland, Houston affiliate of ISA Bank," wrote The Commercial Bank of West Florida.

"We are now in business, based in Rock Bottom, KY., for effective Monday through Friday London bank opening, card trading only, no merchant accounts, C.P.O banking only, no e-money, no f*****, in addition to whatever unofficial custom Spanish or Portuguese new cows get upon riding the political dong. More HSBC everywhere!!"

"Orders take 10 days to come through Europe, 10 the USA. Perfect timing, we are the champions of truth, realism, currency bliss, and the free market. Nothing better than a commercial bank telling you what to do."

George Reid smiled; life was good.

"I call them desk tourers, I guess; they come to foment the flame, set it on fire, and pick up the pieces." Ajira rolled her eyes.

"Well said, toxic!"

Falmouth "The bird market is the most amazing thing I've ever seen; honestly, I love dragons and spearmint water. No, seriously." Jenkyn grimaced as she looked to the east. In the eastern sky, a tiny white dot burned a bright orange. The internet lit up with craziness; pundits sputtered their banshees and telephoned in increased premiums. Groucho wanted a new lease on life, and put his bank account on hold; you could hear rumblings in the caller ID, you wouldn't believe it; JPMorgan was going to explode. Pete wanted to hammer the res — they weren't going to last; Bern's turn was coming soon.

Everything changed in the blink of an eye. Coins were going crazy, and everyone was talking about the Swiss bank account.

Isla Lucia was going to Iceland for the holidays; everyone is going to heaven except for me. I was too broke to feed the animals, and they were going to eat me up. Maha met me on the deck with a stack of quarters, and we went to work. She fried an egg and made a pie, sandwich, and salad. I was starving. I wanted to scream as I picture Jackie Collins hitting the jackpot at the Optimum; I walked out to grab a hot dog from the ottoman, but Teo's mobster father showed up before I could get to Jackson. Dad gave me a hard stare, and walked away; I followed his mini-van with my eyes wide open.

"What the hell is going on with these casinos?'

The sun was setting as I walked down the street; I hated the heat. In the parking lot of the Hilton, I stopped to take a picture of the women's cars, multicolored for the perils of the niqab.

Hell, hath no fury as a camera grabbed in the looks, and Twitter accounts purporting to represent nature. Mt. Gox, the lead currency trader, suddenly lost all of his friends. VanillaTrade, the alt. currency pioneer, went a wee bit crazy, buying up all the newly created iPhones and Bibles. Every evangelist he met was telling him to keep selling bonds and crappy Italian guys with Maserati paying for the institution of Heaven. Maxísion, Tsai's favorite choice of fanciers, made him the butt of jokes across the pond. Cynicism took root as well. Isla Lucia stood by stunned, staring into the abyss of history. It was corporate America, baby, sucker new boys club!

Rupee jumped, hard. Daisies were greener, it was Tuesday, and lakes along the Rhine are warmer. Ciao, Cokes, and Powerade.

Walking to the TV, I fixed the LED on the DOST−15 and set the faceplate black. Computers moved slow; I ran a heads up, that every fucking Dynco video monitor I see today has Java activated. Through the main entrance, I was greeted with gunfire.

"Where's the Army?"

Grisham stood at the front of the line, looking ruder than he had in years. Strong arms, thick beards, and dangerous colored hard hats kept pulling at his jeans. Wearing Navy offense green (something I associate with gambling), two hats hung off his head. Max stood on the other side and introduced the host. Gold sit is the new black, maybe not so bad if you live in the South, but Manhattanites have a different philosophy. It was pitchforks and torches in the air as soon as they got close. Sandbags were thrown, pictures were taken, and scores of legal tender notes slapped on the screen.

Skimming the website for Assassin's Creed, I recalled conversations with members of the London planning committee who invited me to lunch. Scrambled eggs, indeed.

"What's up, dude?"

"Relax; I've got another call an hour ago from the CCPD." He received a rush from the fire hydrant; he hit the pushbutton for the megaphone, and a spokesperson for the division of investigations and operations answered the phone.

"They found your apartment through some traditional plumbing, without a doubt."

"Not much to go on really, I was sleeping a lot of the time; Brian set up a Forex account for me to make payments at 3:30 in the morning when the market opens the fuck up."

"2 for 2, no doubt."

"How about a drink?"

"Guys, let's go; I'm on Facebook."

Chapter 2

I limp lazily behind an exasperated junior. The instructor shook his head as he looked at the air meter; he waved the pen furiously, and with one smooth motion, issued breathless announcements all over the assembled TV cameras. Glass half-full, sky blue as ever.

Civil Engineer phoned up and asked what the problem was. I told him to come in; he was getting on my bad side. He finally went to the room and got my radio on, and oh boy, was I glad he did; it was Planet Tipping, the best trading room I have ever seen. It was packed with the elite traders, including Grønlik, the one with the iron butt.

"Oh my god," Grønlik says.

"What are they up to? I wanted to chill with them. I tell him to fuck off and leave me alone."

"Just checking on the status."

"Swiss bank, a couple of hundred thousand; no problems."

"Can we trade some Ether?"

"Sure, hit the key."

"Just what we need."

"Lots of pairs interested, including the Asians."

"All right guys, it's going to be a lot of trading, we're going to underperform a little bit, but I'm glad to see the market is starting to turn around."

Brooks Walker, the court captain, made some strong plays. You may remember him from his everlasting cameo on The Pros; he was the prize of the trade, at least according to the computer.

"Tell Warren to come back and lick my—" Judge gestured to Brooks.

"Wait a minute, Polkadot is watching from the window, he sees everything!"

"Well, hello again," Dragoon said as he adjusted his gold chain.

"How is the life of the court temperature?"

"Like a bar of iron, no doubt."

"Not much of a temp, usually."

"When is the beginning of lunch?"

"The middle of the night, probably."

"So, what is the matter?"

"They saw my Atticus sign and started talking to me," Beloved One continued.

"You fool!" Crusader threw his arms up in the air.

The sky darkened, and raining winds blew scraps of paper at the windows, repeatedly. The Wankeks sitting in the inn's jacuzzi demanded to be "flashed," lest they get snot on their boots. Spoiled brats. Pucci sat in the courtyard drinking Limoncello. For once in his miserable life, Comerio felt guilty; he walked inside, made some fake banking records look more legit, and posted a $10 bill on the jalousie window.

"Are you sure this thing is going to work?" Sumi typed.

"Trust me, this is going to explode in a minute," I typed back.

"It gives me the creeps just to look at the damn chart."

"Don't screw things up or you're going to miss the momentum. Either jump in at the signal, or stay out," typed Goldmine.

"It's a lot of money. I never traded a single lot; all I did was the micro, 8,000 units at max, up to yesterday," Sumi replied.

"That's pussy trading," typed MonsterMind.

The chat room was getting animated.

"Hey guys, what happened to ForexSuckers or whatever was the name of that new dealer?" Sizzler asked.

"The other day I was in with twenty lots and the freakin' system started going nuts. My orders got closed at market, I think they did it. After that, they shut down for the day."

"Twenty lots?"

"They probably freaked out," typed Monstermind.

"I don't care if they don't want my business, heck with them. I'll play somewhere else."

"Yeah, teach these sissies how it's done," typed Pipette, the Chinese superstar. "You burned 'em out, I'm quite sure. "

"What I like about Oanda is that you trade any amount and they never blink an eye."

"I like them too; they put the regular folks, like us and the big banks all in the same pot."

"Yeah, that's classy."

"How many lots have you traded with them in a single shot?"

"Forty."

"Forty lots?"

"Yeah bro', forty big fat lots."

"What's that, just for quick math?"

"100,000 times forty."

"Shit!"

"I was trading the US dollar against the Swiss franc, and all of a sudden it was on fire, ka-Ching, ka-Ching, ka-Ching! I was laughing hard, my stomach hurt. Better than anything you'll ever experience. My girl kept yelling, 'Would you stop looking at the damn monitor and come to the room and fuck me?' I told her to get lost; she hasn't talked to me since."

"All right guys, it's moving."

"Send the signal!"

Place market order at 1. 3766 no stop loss (SL), take profit (TP) at 1. 3810, trade at your own risk.

"Let's go, folks, let's go!"

"Yeah, it's going to skyrocket!"

"Fuck DB (Deutsche Bank), fuck it! Go suck my tamale, and tell the other suckers from now on to keep selling bonds, and jack up the rates."

"Economists my ass. You can't keep up with us, we are now the center of gravity of the Forex market. We are the revolution. It's no longer you, suck-up bankers who control the world currency, you're fuckin' doomed. Capisce?"

SureLess Social Strategy Report division annual press briefing addressed to the sets teams "Here's what you need to know"—presumably calculating off the trailing 10% of the trading volume. Of note: JPM quotes 65.18 as

T BANDITS

its dedicated trading threshold, TVF calls up their banking expert with some serious air quotes.

The weather was starting to turn, top sided beads of perspiration on clubfoot and paper currency at the ready. Traders can also get sucked into a frenzy when the tropical sun comes up, chanced upon a peripheral component or two and can't resist splashin' the pool. There was bound to be some action around dress code, e-wear code... it didn't matter, we were bonkers.

At least Konstantin considered us harmless when preparing quotas for Monday markets; it's always hell on earth out there on the oil patch. Worry not, America! We came prepared! Go ahead with your bank accounts opened this week and flush the toilet.

If you haven't noticed, I've been tinkering in the corner getting into bitcoin better known to the tourist crowd. Bitcoin badass. XCP high strength. All that prick crap. Quick response times even quicker. Silk road or bust. VISA unless you give me extra instructions. Whatever, I am here to meet you with good intentions. Meet Richard, invite him to an evening of cheap Lübeck beer and daiquiri, of course. Bitcoin!!!

Gentlemen like Mandell tend to see eye-to-eye on gender politics. A once thriving Chinese crypto financial center with a gentle demeanor allowed sex and debauchery to quietly prosper. Eventually, fashion wore thin and thievery discovered a marketable skill in carbon copy—a decadent custom of the tradesman. It worked: quantity dropped precipitously. Gentlemen preferring beer and grins don't mix. Chances are good, trade this dress code and settle for Sakaki Gourmet Ramen or junk food and pitchers of caustic soda. A happy incident; Visa refusing to honor CNY (Yuan) was the only greeting. Barbarians!

China became nervous; I'll get to them in a minute; for now, just check out the tank, obviously full of fried chicken.

By the way, things never get old between China and the west, right?

Fish catch rates top out at about 10 million a year. Translation: a little bit better than average. Way up there. Break-even? It could be worse. Prices aren't much of an issue in the tropics. People shop at the inopportune time. In Puerto Rico, for example, there is a sixty percent black market for everything from refrigerators to rickshaws. Restaurants eat an up-regulation portion and squeeze out more revenue by getting brusquely indifferent to their drunken customers. Pay as you go! Barbarism! Freakin' cool!

Don't call them Africans, please! It's more offensive than they know; they think gypsies move the currency. Then there is 'Nair ant yeh aabuchadià,' the indigenous spirit prevalent in Judea, Aruba, and the Caribbean Islands. Young people are buying saucy phrases and popular songs on bandpass. Often dance parties decked out in traditional Egyptian garb. Ask any Islamic scholar any question and he will just respond in French. Not bad for a private consultation.

Chapter 3

"Today I smoked two packs of Gauloises, threw on my slippers and jersey shore gear, and—Gotta love the weather here in the tropics—went to the casino. Not too shabby."

The Boss stared at the monitor. He adjusted the contrast and scratched his head. After a minute, he pulled out a conga stick and started beating the drum for a change.

"Hey Guys" he started yelling. Guys, listen up!"

"Hmm..."

Two young men from DigiTD walked by. They exchanged a look and gave each other a stare.

"How is trading? Are the indexes anywhere near last week's levels?"

"Not great."

"I wanted to send my condolences, but I didn't think anybody would take the bait."

"I didn't think they would," I replied.

"I told them that I'll see what I can do; if they shirk their responsibility, I'll send a cease and desist letter to their email addresses." The Boss snorted as he looked over to the right.

"Let's go guys; let's go!"

"Yeah, it's going to skyrocket!"

Girls looked up to the right.

"Yeah, it is," replied Oakley.

"Did you read the news?" Asked Kaiser.

"I haven't," replied Kilman.

"The bank got crushed badly."

"I thought we had the upper hand on these cockroaches."

"Doesn't look like it."

"How can a handful of day traders disrupt the market like that?"

"Don't call them day traders, they hate the label."

"What are they?"

"Forex traders; apparently a different breed."

"Cockroaches, that's what they are."

"Probably that's the reason they multiply so fast; we need more glue traps."

"You're overreacting."

"Overreacting my ass."

"They just got lucky a few times, that's all."

"We've got half dozen of the Eurozone countries complaining to the central bank, and the central bank asking us what the hell we're doing with the trades."

"So, what?"

"The currency is trading too high and they're paranoid."

"Tell them to come and trade, then; let's see how good they are at the game."

"We are the market makers, we have unlimited resources, according to them."

"We are not market makers. These stupid professors in economics turned bureaucrats know nothing about the Forex; they think we're trading crack."

"I know, but who is going to explain it to them?"

"This market is too big; it makes Wall Street look like the chicken and sausage stand on Moreland Avenue."

Kaiser shook his head and lit up a cigarette.

"Remember ten years ago the SOES bandits?"

"Yeah, I wanted to be one of them."

"They didn't last very long. The market makers could see anything they were up to, and always play some nasty tricks on them; they finally burned out."

"It was politics."

"That too. The moral of the story, this market is way different. No more market makers, everybody on the same boat."

"That's right."

"The countries that are complaining about the currency going up too much should finally wake up, smell the flowers, not each other's derriere, and become more competitive."

"It's going to take years."

"What about Germany? When they had the Mark, it was strong and they kept growing and growing."

"They believe it's hard to compete with China, India, and Brazil whose currency is worth nothing."

"Just tell 'em to keep selling bonds, to pay for the pensionati, as they call them in Italy.

Alfonso Borello

Chapter 4

Costa Mesa, CA – Civic Auditorium – Ageist Fantasy Water Music Festival – 96,965 People.
Great venue, no doubt, but unfortunately, no one paid attention until the intrepid sportswriter from ProFootß stumbled on the show two days before it started. Brea Andreas, Cleveland's beloved former naval stooge of Rachel's Addiction, was giving a sold-out convention a motivational lecture, it seemed. Pastor Topeka, Georgia's second most popular preacher, had just finished delivering an 8-hour sermon, the drones stopped dead on the King James and everyone just sat there, curious as to which of the '80s bankrolled derangement this sweaty retro looked guy was going to liken it to. Question is, who is going to preach to the slobbering babies? Praise God!
One of the cameras cut away to reveal a ridiculously tall businessman dressed in black wearing a Red Sox cap and sitting on the freaking television. Red Sox merchandise was re-released two weeks ago, by eBay connoisseur Daisuke Ohkoshi, you might recall. The image was projected on eleven gals wrapped with white

T BANDITS

beach towels, en Español. The quality was pretty mediocre by Japanese standards, but the delivery was impeccable. Pretty soon 90% of the sellers were back online, as expected. Working 99 cents trade, most coupons turned good. Expensive items make terrible sellers, tag your Luke Mary, or worse. The shirt featured Bustin' Madonna and champions.

Commercial break.

△ △ △

CLEVELAND – JUNE 19 – IBIS.com, the electronic banking joint venture of Germany's DAX and France's Paris of course, gave us some bad news today. The operators of the Galbraith bank in Cleveland reported that one of their biggest customers was under legal investigation for tax fraud. James Galbraith
was widely referred to in the press for his stellar record managing pension funds, the Four Seasons, the Fox, Sumlin's, NW Auto, FIAT and what we now know as JPMorgan.
   Ten minutes later, the Journal hit the clubs. Who among us didn't want to be photographed holding the Journal for the bankers?
   Worse, we discovered, the generator that powers the club had mysteriously exploded. London is burning, and we're the only ones who can put out the flame. Rent is skyrocketing, and nobody seems to care.
   Why did they do that?
   Our first thought was that it's a Red Giant thing. The seat of the Butterfly? Anchors down.

We looked at the 6 AM local time gauge . . . still trading too low, I could feel it . . . hot.

What about Brooklyn?

Where's it at?

Our finger fell on the subhead of the article: FOREX DAY TRADERS HIT THE JACKPOT AGAIN. CARDIAC CONTESTS HAVEN'T LOSERS, NO REPORTS HAVE COME IN SOUTHERN LEAN ASIA I'M UNDERSTANDAAARD.

Two leads we followed--the biz while was going to punish the suckers with losses equal to 350 million AUD, or $65 billion, and it was going to be on TV.

"What about the advertisers?" I asked.

"They're lining up to switch to French since they hate the f-k anaerobic workouts; according to one high-profile French neophyte, they are even shooting pool."

"All right, bravo, sucker-pant, now it's personal.

"What should I tell them?"

"That they should meet me in the club at the lively O2, Queen's balcony."

The indoor pool was pretty hipper than the outdoor, greener Sophia's apartment preferred, the bill placed higher by artist-invitees. There were a couple of dozen suit-and-tie conservatives milling about, mostly dressed for the occasion.

"This is going to be great," Olla said as she entered.

"I need a cab; 630; they fix the euro."

"Take one, 312 WIND GENT, they talk fast."

The Wall Street Journal hit the newsstand at four in the morning; I was awake as always, the market begins in Asia around midnight, rather mildly, but at three in the morning Eastern time, London wakes up and my monitors are bright enough to keep me awake. Pots of coffee through an I.V. regulate the adrenaline. I didn't need to get out in the cold to grab a copy, I typed AsianTimes.com and read the clone of the very same article on the Journal: FOREX DAY TRADERS HIT THE JACKPOT AGAIN. The subhead read: Euro too high (red fonts). Banks and institutions on their knees.

Beautiful. I had to read the damn article five times. I was getting high. The green dot on the chat room blinked.

"Read the article?" Goldmine asked.

"Going for the sixth time, unless you want to sing it to me," I replied.

"I'm going to rap it in the morning. Gotta friend downtown who's got real talent; I'll throw him a bucket of fried chicken, and he'll sing anything for me."

"You're nuts."

"I'm fuckin' serious; I'll even send an mp3 to the president of the ECB; he's going to love it."

"What's going on today?"

"I read somewhere the banks are going to take extreme measures to fight back, and put the Euro back where it should be."

"They have no idea."

"Right. Got new recruits by the way."

"How many?"

"About 1,500."

"Sweet."

"We've got about 800 last week alone."

"That explains the spike."

"I only count 1,200 and above. Anything less leaves me totally indifferent."

"If they listen and don't chicken out, they can make some serious money."

"Some can't handle it."

"You're damn right."

"They see all that money blinking on their screen, probably some might even have a heart attack."

"The Asians are the best; they've got gambling in their blood; they love the chop-chop feeling."

"The Patels and Guptas are getting better, but I find them a little bit too conservative."

"Not too found on them, personally; they like the stock better, slow pace."

"Ready for the attack?"

"I'm in bro'. Send the go!"

Trade 10 lots market order at 1. 3901 no SL, set auto TP at 1. 3987, trade at your own risk. Champagne after hitting the target; Mylanta for the pussies.

I smelled food on the stove, I pressed play on the radio and was given the go-ahead to check. There wasn't a thing. Nothing but fucking meatballs, that's for sure. There wasn't anything else on the TV either, it was G4C standards. There was no code to set it apart from the others, they all looked the same.

"So, where's the fucking beach?" He asked.

They weren't being serious, they were joking around.

"It's on da dais, CENTURION STABIRMUS ."

They weren't amused.

"Cut it out, stooge!"

They walked on.

"Where?" They asked.

"The fucking Hilton."

"Hotel."

"Can we stay in the room?"

"We can. Get your room ticket at the desk."

"This is way out in the country, right?"

They walked on.

"Out in the cold?"
They guessed.
"Out in the cold with the flu?"
They guessed again. More than they'd ever seen before.
"How about a cold beer?"
"Two pitchers from the GI bank."
They ordered a cab and set off for downtown.
"Fort Worth is a big place to make a killing."
"How?"
They looked up the G4C.
"Visit the Nine Tigers headquarters, find out how to Jack the Stocks, and sweetheart lucrative bonuses."
"Forty-nine two, Houston, Texas."
"Forty-Seventh Street, on the other side of the canal."
"I don't think I've seen that street much in the last couple of years," said Rosa as she stared at the skyscrapers.
They soon discovered that it wasn't just the banks that were sweating the ankle, it was the entire planet. Human civilization seemed to have one too many pancake houses, and it was starting to look like the Asian Tigers were going to have the last laugh.

Alfonso Borello

Chapter 5

Honorable Mention: StarCityBrokers.com
Fact: Rockstar Games! Woah! Of all the bitcoin taggers out there, I find them rather amusing. Jingling keys on a CV? Too bad. Ka-Ching.
Banksafe "GO HOUR!!" "8:57"
Shrimp boil every five minutes. Drain well, treat it like cooked rice. For real.
"Where should we put our orders?"
Waist-high in the air, and sporting a gleaming BMW badge, Tiger Mamas Mahim blinked. Gets on the self-checkout machines, and hits the jackpot. Citibank comes up with the bird, Goldmine the pinkie, and everyone is happy. Bank accounts light up with XCF at 7%. All personnel at the center of the cross is smiling. Fitness king Mike Fox spends the afternoons in the city, slapping the same walk as, figuring he's got some elite Swindon hands on him. Financial Times again! Not sure if I'm smiling anymore. Stick to the cards Pete. Cute profile in the FT? I thought so. The top will hit the club in two days. Plan B. Business as usual at the center of the inferno. Rome dam to the world! Traffic jam at the

T BANDITS

Harbor, Mon mediesta! Chiampsé of Switzerland set to trade. Traffic light.

Inside Barclays, Winston was staring at the Fox News, the Terresa Palmer show on CNBC, and Hindsight is 20/20 about all that. Still couldn't fall asleep. Hustling for a Hong Kong TA, I picked up Chi called up at the office. He greeted me with a quick 200-yuan bill and handed me a gaokao in Chinese.

A professional-looking guy with dreads kept walking to the door. A friendly face, dark eyes, narrow shoulders, and cropped blue jeans. Brake lights flashing. The store-brand Indian red dirham was his cue to chat. He gaveled the door with brute force, dragged it closer, and cursed vulgarity is country code for mon ami. Rak Ma Sword Holy Grail! Foam paddles whistled. Shrimp fried rice and beans soup was his oyster. Steak tartare was his columbo. Tailgaters danced politely. Dress code: black.

"I uncover!?" Madame complained.

He scratched his head and imagined, again. "I found it on Labyrinthine Research, two guys using economics as a vice; marketing as such, they installed agent provocateurs. Source .05 %. 08 IBM stock average .073 NADA maximum — exchange rate manual moderate 3 R300 margin, trades each other near 100000000."

Madame looked up and gave him a hard stare.

"What do you want to know?" She asked.

He scratched his head, and OTTCANC opened his Excel spreadsheet.

ECB headquarters, Frankfurt, Germany.

"Mr. President, everybody's in the conference room for the meeting; they're waiting for you," said the secretary.

"I'm on the other line, tell them to piss on the sidewalk, I'll be there in a minute," the president replied as he tapped on the intercom.

"This won't take much of your time," he started.

"We're here to listen, Mr. President," the French representative replied; he drummed his fingers on the table a couple of times.

"We've got a problem," the president continued, "these folks are getting on my nerves."

"They are getting on everybody's nerves," said Shultz, the German banker from DB.

"We have to deal with the problem, these guys are not going away," interrupted Bisset, the French.

"You're right, they are not going away, but we can inflict some pain if we have to," a voice shouted.

"We're in Frankfurt here, inside a prestigious institution, we don't practice and we don't encourage waterboarding," the official sitting by the window replied.

A sudden burst of disapproval erupted in the room and was just the beginning.

"The currency is too high, and we're not going to have a bunch of canailles to disrupt our budgets," the Greek premier shouted.

"Well, you should have known better yourself a few years back when you borrowed the money you couldn't pay back, with those crappy Olympics you hosted, which of course ran your country to the ground," replied the Portuguese.

"You should know better before insulting me, your country can only exist because of your neighbor, and now that they cut you off, I'm really curious to see who you're going to call; Brazil perhaps?"

The Spanish representative was sitting on the other end of the table, registered the innuendo, and gave them a solid look.

"Gentlemen, please," the president interrupted.

Two walked away, the Turkish looked around and set a miniature hookah on the table. The sallow man sitting next to him shook his head and blanched.

"I'm going to adjourn the meeting for next Wednesday; hopefully someone will bring some fresh ideas to the table,"

Business as usual at the ECB?

Chapter 6

Sure, typically five zeros for five revolutions tanks?! VFFC pol? Facts are damned" Screamed National Mayor Joe Hong, standing in the rain near headquarters.

I answered them by tapping on their cellular. Compulsion!!

Exiting here?" Gasps emerged from 10 of the places occupying my feeder. Cool!" Polo wanted to know where I was headed.

Investing?" Buenzilli retorted.

Maybe in California."

Or in London." Buyer beware." Sell order taken." Sell at price! They raise the bar too high! Die with pride!" The mutual fund manager advised.

Fair enough. Trade channels congested optimum limits waived." Collect my draw." PayPal can't handle these kinds of transactions anymore." Domain names are bouncing." Embrace the shorts! Commuters and tourists from different parts of the globe staring at their bank statements. . .

Dealers are wiring the Band-Aids, the sore losers from the currency war. Bars and restaurants in Zürich are sporting no fixed signs of activity, and all eyes are on the television set at home."

Transit systems north of Boston will probably stay open all night, barring an unprecedented accident. Up until now, customers from New York or Los Angeles have generally been good about modifying schedules, unless otherwise directed by extortionate cab fares. ÜSavior Spain sent word through the united prostitute corps to watch what they're doing here in the USA," a young woman wearing an air horn explained. She racked her brains a few times, before choosing between which airline to subscribe to. Berlin was probably more opportune for a little tut-tutting, she surmised. She sighed and clicked on the cancel travel button.

Germany's about ready to go for fuck's sake!" Berita added with a grin. Rules?!"

E-business here going?! Que dais tu my ballade?" One of the clerks asked with his blue-chipped bijou ahead of him.

Don't be silly, sir, only bus and train from here on out. Don't expect cheaper rounds of Mario or whatever."

"You're kidding me!"

"Of course, I'm fucking kidding you. I'm just here to collect your kickback, you know?"

"Aren't you curious?"

"So, do I, naturally. Although when I picked up your cab today, I was expecting Cologne to have kicked ass. Passengers arriving earlier were asking how long they were going to be sitting on the train, and I could see the annoyance on their faces. Since so many from Asia are sending chill vibes, I figured I'd play some Hostess, too." Strumpet, no less!

Since last time I checked on Portland's western border, cars have been speeding. Massive speeding cars!" Anyway, I warned them about the crazy thermals; they ignored me.

"Put the throttles back in neutral, and let's go traffic cop!" Demolish the car, seize the damn truck, stop traveling the wrong way, embrace speed limit signs and summon girls to call the cops on them."

Last week, the Consul from India featured prominently on our channel.

Nandan Nilekani is from Dharamsala, in northeast India, quite a distance from where we are.

"My name is Dr. William Krueger, a good reputation agent from KY home server speaking from the heart." The reporter from SCMP asked, waving his compoess, plate and registered letters; always refreshing BSR's analytics system. Lots of interaction and crappiness, purveyors of truth and medicine.

"If there's any industry subject you're unfamiliar with, show up tomorrow morning to be featured on the show, okay?" Dr. Krueger nodded, straightening out his fine silk tie. "Sure, what kind of a guest are you?" SY Loser interrogates.

△ △ △

Washington, D. C., United States, Federal Reserve headquarters – 9:17 local time.

"So, what's up in the old continent?" Asked the Chairman.

"Same old, too old to make things happen, which of course is good for us, no doubt," replied the Vice-Chairman.

"What's the problem?"

"They can't keep the currency at bay, it just hit the milky way and about to reach the North Star; I just checked the monitor."

"What do they want us to do?"

"According to their investigation, there's a large group of underground traders who are the trouble makers."

"Nonsense."

"They want us to check on these guys."

"What are we supposed to do? Bring them to justice?"

"Exercise pressure, sort of."

"I don't see anything wrong about trading."

"According to an independent French investigation, they're using unethical business practices to scout new traders."

"I don't get it."

"Neither do I. they tell the newbies how to trade."

"Now I'm even more confused," the Chairman retorted. He raised his gaze to the ceiling.

"They use a chat room; one gives the signal and the peloton acts according to the cryptic."

The Chairman rolled his eyes.

"Are you still there?"

"Yes, I need a drink, but I think I'll settle for another coffee; this comedy show is amusing, definitely French."

"They want us to go after the leaders of the chat room."

"Are you serious?"

"Yes, I've got another call an hour ago from Frankfurt."

"The ECB?"

"Yes, they have intelligence that the masterminds are here in the US."

"Too bad."

"I told them that I'll see what I can do; of course, I didn't mention a thing."

"If they feed Uncle Sam, there isn't much we can do."

"I'll double-check on that, just out of curiosity. If you don't mind, of course."

"I wouldn't move a finger."

"So, what am I going to tell 'em?"

"That they need to get their act together, and stop pointing fingers. There's no case. These are independent traders, and if they don't break any law, there's nothing we can do."

"Can we just pretend that we're doing our part?"

"Sure. Tell them to kick out Greece and send it back to the drachma or boiled peanuts, and institute more rigorous eligibility to join the club next time. No more Greek tragedies, please."

"Sounds like a plan, chief."

"Whatever."

Chapter 7

NEW SEPERATION: ICO (Initial Coin Offer) GHOST LAKE

Having just returned from exploring the depths of China's unregulated cryptocurrency market, I came across an interesting story. Having never heard of such a bubble, I was quite surprised to find out that there was a market for it. I had no idea what to make of it. Still, I kept digging and digging and discovered that it was quite popular, at least in China. Their heroes are always fighting for market share, I am told. According to a reputable source who I shall not name, there is even a vending machine where you can pay cash for square inches of toilet paper, shampoo, soap, and cosmetic treatments. Interesting.

Anyway. Since Chinese internet connections are unfortunately notoriously poor, we needed good ol' fashioned Chinese help. So, we sent an email to a chat room service known as WeChat, which means answer both ends with hi and fa. To my utter amazement, both Gao and Leeteuk replied in Chinese.

"Hello again, Gallant. It's Gao from the chat room. I changed my numbers, now please come back to the chat room. Will do."

Heck yeah. Chinese sex chat rooms at their finest.

On the condition of anonymity, I used Myspace to befriend the devil.

Technical details aren't important; it all goes by Myspace tags. Log off, log in, and hit the forward button. A giant yellow arrow will pop up; click it seven times.

Once you've hit the forward button more times, you'll see some humor images pop up.

"I confirm receipt of your message."

"Keep sending?"

"You bet!"

"Yeah, right."

"Cool!"

Below is an image macro sent in by brandnewb, a funny guy from Chicago. It's still visible on his wall.

WeChat-Fu the grass is always greener on the other side, right?" He typed.

"What's up today?"

"Catch the mic from Frank Punato, the preacher at Hong Kong's Pilatus publicity center."

△ △ △

Designer Bio

[Sports Writer] Signpost? Hajime umm, yeah, kind of worrying. Miss IEM, is this her? Good. Damn she's sharp. Not like those Chinese midgets at work too much these days. [Click to enlarge] Shop around a little bit, I

guess. Might want to lighten up on the pro-am stuff a little bit. Ok, sorry. Let's talk business.
Hi!

△ △ △

Beijing, China – 7:37 AM
Inside the offices of the Central Reserve Bank of China, an exceptionally tall businessman dressed in black was giving a presentation holding a copy of The New Forex Times, a local influential paper on currency and commodity trading. More than a presentation it smelled like a press conference; the attendance was beyond expectation, and the enthusiasm was exorbitant; one reporter showed up with his wife and a little boy who kept munching on a wooden bowl of shrimp fried rice #2049.

The tall man worked the crowd with talent; he waved the paper with divination and moved his finger across the headline, while one of the television cameras zoomed in. The image was projected on a 500 plus-inch LED screen, made in China with Japanese parts. He read the headlines twice and then moved his finger, which had a chipped nail, on the subhead and screamed, "Financial markets in shambles. Euro too high. Commercial banks and dealers on their knees."

It was more than plagiarism, it was a carbon copy of the headline published by the Wall Street Journal just the week before; it wasn't typed in simplified Chinese, it was a medley of Mandarin and ancient Cantonese, and cleverly decorated with unique purfles, to make it look more original.

The little kid had just finished his snack and gave a high five to the tall man. The father was getting irritated because the record button on his tiny device jammed, and had to hit violently his wife with his elbow for pen and paper. She gave him a hard stare, reached in her purse, and pulled out a fortune cookie.

△ △ △

Zhucheng, southeast of Shandong, 315 miles south of Beijing. Cornucopia numero uno; it's the freakin' Chip'n Dale, poster boy. A Compromise, that is. Money talks; no one is ever going to subvert the throne. Pots of coffee through an Imperial China draft windmill complicate the calculus even further.
"How much did they put in?"
"About what we're making it."
"Pretty much what we were expecting; some guinea-fondlers, that is."
"How many tons are we buying?"
"Forty tons."
"Forty tons." Nice work, everybody."
"We've got half a billion dollars of inventory, that's proper."
"We didn't break a finger, except for one; that was a ninja breakage," said major Hu Wen, the captain of the police.
"What did they say?"
"Don't tell 'em," I replied.
"We're going back to the office and repairing all the fucks up," said sergeant Mao Zun, the deputy superintendent of police.

"You're not wasting my time," said the president.
"I'm going to raid their offices," and check the books. They will not be having any of that," said the judge.
"So, what am I going to tell 'em?"
"Don't tell 'em," I replied.
"You've got a bomb on your hands, you're lucky I didn't drop something suspicious on your face."
"Don't tell me that the Chinese Communists used your own countrymen as guinea pigs?"
"It's a long story; I found out the hard way."
"If they did, I might just have a true friend north of the box."
"Let me check on that," I said as I walked away.

Tracking idols, card-based trading, investing, chat room, more, smiles, nice shot!

Preflight check-in was quick and painless, the J.C. makes my dick pop like a Vicodin; I was set for the day at 7:27 AM, it was going to be a lot of fucking CNY shopping, a nice TV for watching the stream, and a casino to burn. Anything to spice things up.

It wasn't so quick. Neaťhe hotel is quite a circus, the AC is bad, the Wi-Fi is intermittent, but everything else is fixed. Red Hot & Angry's Tang Fandong soundtrack played on the little hookah table in the room. The hostess dressed in a sexy swim triton walked Jack Ma to a den and gave him a massage.

Chapter 8

"I was merely curious as to make an investment, and sell at a profit... was it nothing at all? Don't worry! Zero kille tak out 'Bout it! :O)"

20th St. SW, Washington, D. Canadian metropolitan area; headquarters to Freemasons.

"Am I supposed to be sad? Hmm, no!" Passionate excitement trumps all. London must've cast some friendly... female Grim eyes.

"Any ideas about what the secret séance is about?"

Pots of coffee, virtual assassins chatting—Toronto time is now 12:32 EST.); Shots of tequila, I gather.

At last!" Emerald kneels to kiss my hand, "Ma'am, may I?"

"Has anyone spotted any signs of Ajay?"

"Nope, pervy as usual."

Former Deputy Chief Counsel Civil Division Edward Eckstein advises against mentioning the case to the White House; by law, he must've known all about it. Unless..."

"Central Bank got wind of it," Ajay replied.

"Nah, nothing to see about it." Confused? Oh no. The economy is booming," founder of the financial advisory firm Younger Hedge Funds Corp. gives off a snort. He points to a Bloomberg's humungous monitor at his side; Chai ran it for him.

"Swap bars?"

"Yeah, what else?"

"Umm... Chinese Yuan, Rupee, and shit like that." He points to the faintest smudge on the grayscale.

"Not much going on these days, I can tell."

"It's probably a bug in the trading software."

"Knock on wood," replies Eisenstein.

"See nothing here, I've been looking the other way."

"Don't be a fool, sir, my people live in caves underneath the Himalayas."

"Right, and the kitchen sinks are on fire," she giggles.

"Guess which way the wind blows today?"

"I don't see anything, that's for sure."

"Fair enough. Time to hit the barn."

"This way please!"

"That's what traders do, man."

"Teachers often kill their students for trying to cheat on tests."

"These people won't last a second longer."

"Don't be foolish," I hear people yelling.

"This market isn't gonna tank, it just got started."

Harold instructs Kaisar to remove his U.S. dollar order at 0.00000155, change wager 10, raise a hand, and trade in bitcoin only. Put your horse before your cow, Johnson.

Ups and downs, man. Swaps are happening. Prices are dropping.

But who is going to tell them how to run the firm? Or what to buy and sell?

It's going to take years to figure out what to do about it. Skilled traders know better. And for what? Big shiny new buildings.

Last time I checked, no country was going to move its currency by printing its new issues of the notorious Stasi economics manual. Or with its currency.

Admittedly I wasn't surprised. Years of training as a card-carrying member of parliament, too many to count, distinguishable by the noose around my neck. Three years ago, Japan finally became a mature civilization. Mortgage defaults went down almost instantly. Regulatory frameworks changed."

In other words, it was business as usual for Japan's bankers. Sort of like Germany two thousand years ago, when they finally elected a government that understood economics. Things didn't get better in Japan, however. Suddenly anti-monetary sentiment is running high, and merchants are starting to panic. One reason is that the Chinese currency is trading too high. Another is that the Japanese central bank is hinting at increased efforts to fight corruption."

Unfortunately for them, money talks.

Of course, not to outsiders like them. Citizens love kings and queens. King-diehards love their golden parachutes. Even Holland elected its first emperor in golden armor." But on a grander scale, no less, as evidenced by King Chassos of India's remarkable run for the crown.

I clicked on the balance of the trading account; I felt a rush of adrenaline which I haven't experienced in years. My first solo landing was a kick, no doubt—but this was something else. My hand was shaking as I hit the request button for the withdrawal—it was fuckin' beautiful.

I felt like going out and spend some of it, but I had to wait two days for the transfer to go through. It was Wednesday and probably won't even show up until Monday; I didn't mind the wait—I was salivating. I wanted to call everyone and tell them to fuck off and stop talking to me; I could no longer be their friend. I suddenly became someone else. Something so terrible happens when you make a little dough. I shook my head.

Is this shit for real? So easy? How long is going to last?

My head started spinning. I knew I had to calm down. I couldn't. Don't blame it on me. It's a money thing. Something so bad. Something so embarrassing even to write about it. Here I am, the new prick on the block with a few dollars on a bank account which has never seen more than a couple of thousand.

What if the IRS is going to call me and ask questions?

I rushed out to get my mail; I grew paranoid. That's what money does. It fucks up your brain.

At least Homo Erectus never had such worries; he was busy killing to feed himself, and, just for fun, killing other men to steal their women and inserting his penis without asking permission.

The phone buzzed. I tapped on the screen; seven Emails. All from the elite traders discussing their shopping list; one bought a pickup truck, one a big screen TV, one an iPad, and the others were consulting with their better half. Soraya felt the need to celebrate; she bought a ticket and was boarding the new A380 Emirates (complete with shower rooms) flight from

London to come to spend the weekend with me in Atlanta.

Chapter 9

"This panel is just to gauge your expectations. We're here to listen and determine if you have any interest in becoming a member. Are you brand new here?" Emilia asked.

"I'm a registered voter."

"Oh my god!"

Later, in the hall, Elizabeth sat at the head of the table reading The Wall Street Journal. She grinned as she read the headlines. One was about Volkswagen cheating on their diesel emissions tests and the other about the manipulated Swiss bank accounts. Her mind was made up; she was going to vote for the chicken.

"They used...alley demons to scout newbies."

Everyone around her was staring at the e-mail; they didn't know what to make of it. "What the hell is going on today?" Goldmine asked.

Murata responded by tapping on the intercom.

"I'm on the Canary front, trying to get some traffic to the site."

"Can you hack into the WIFI at the hotel and bring the traffic to a crawl?"

Cramped under the load of the Internet, Jessica rewound the clock and set it to HH:MM.

"Of course."

Five hours later she got an e-mail from the secret Twitter bot that gave her the traffic.

"A reminder to tune in at 7 for the chat!" Skipped the break for lunch.

"Tune in, Ma'am!" Cantor ordered.

Utterly stupefied, the cable TV provider set her fixer legs and left her fuming on the carpet. She stormed out to the street, clawing her hands with both her feet. Clouded by the dew, she made her way to a local sandwich shop, bought a can of Heinz beans and fresh-squeezed Mets. She finally made it back to the house, sat on the porch and set the doorknob a second time.

The light was soft outside. She knocked on the front door. Three times. Nothing.

Her heart sank as she remembered the conversation with the djinn a few days back. She hit the back of the phone five times, but there was no response. Lucky for her, it was the high school, basketball team. No matter. She phoned them and made them coffee; she got them to come out to watch. She watched from the monitor as her target opponent, the all-time scoring champ Wu Xun pushed his way to the center of the court. The green dot on the court was surrounded by orange and blue. Every move he made was preceded with a crunch. He pushed the ball up and down with uncanny agility. It was crazy.

Piotr Judański was sitting on the court wearing a red and white striped referee's jersey. Around him were clustermunks of yellow and green hues, juggling balls of some sort. All kinds of complicated things were playing basketball, replete with shooting and passing. Apparently, Piotr was the guru. His pupils are now A's, a first for Europe.

Cantor walked over to Piotr and patted his hand.

"You done set something on fire, paddy?"

"Yeah, I set the whole thing on fire. It's got smoke and mirrors everywhere."

"How much longer is going to last?"

He scratched his head and scratched his head many, many more times.

Cantor pulled out a paper napkin and began to write.

"We've got about an hour before the game starts."

He fiddled with the lights in the room for a minute, and they blinked a couple of times.

Shit! The Light Eater Inn is back! Hoo boy. Stink up, Fuego."

"You're damn right."

"We're not looking to get seated, just the playing field. Stick to the game and you'll never cross paths with the West Coast armed forces again."

Seated at the counter, Ramone Khaled the officer on the lookout for Eichmann looked up to see Citrine sitting by the window smoking a cigarette. Crocodile-chipped, it was.

Fortune smiled upon him again as he pulled out his mobile and dialed the Frankfurt international airport. On the other end of the line was an AIG rep, asking what the hell he was doing in the rain. Ten thousand he actually meant to pay for a new bridge, right? Verrrra – date! Bag on Wheels!

Citrine smiled and hurried off to get his suitcase, the Swiss Army.

I picked up Soraya at the airport; she was wearing a sports outfit and, to my surprise, had only one carry-on bag. She looked much younger compared to the profile picture in the chat room.

"Alfonso, finally I can see you live," she greeted me with a firm handshake.

"It's about time," I replied.

"How about dinner?" She asked.

"You're not tired?"

"I slept the whole trip. I'm hungry."

"All right. Let's drop your bag at my place first."

"No need; my hotel is just a mile from here."

"Let's go," I said.

"Do you mind if I drive?" She asked.

"I don't. I can't stand driving; I can't wait to put my hands on one of those Google cars."

The drive ended up being three miles; she wasn't light on the pedal.

"Ten minutes," she said.

I lounged on the easy chair in the hall. One of the TV hanging had CNBC on, but nobody bothered with it.

She was ready in no time. Red dress, black boots above the knee, and so much jewelry to make you wonder how everything fits in that small bag.

"I called the front desk and they told me there's a great place inside the hotel, Spice Market, I believe," Soraya said.

"So much the better," I replied.

She walked ahead of me; she had charisma and a sense of urgency.

"Two for a nice dinner; kind of business-like, a quite table please," Soraya instructed.

The hostess nodded and stared at Soraya's boots, "British accent?" She asked.

"I'm not British, but I live in London," Soraya replied.

"This way please."

"This is a little bit too dark," I complained.

"It's fine. Don't worry, I won't bite," said Soraya as she gestured to the hostess.

"All right, finally on earth again," she said as she adjusted her peacock earrings.

"Soraya, nice outfit!" I said as I looked down.

She smiled and patted my hand.

"Who polishes your boots?"

She shook her head, "Nobody yet."

"Hmm. . ."

"Al, stop it!"

"All right, let's get into character."

"Do you know why I was such in a hurry to come to see you?" Soraya asked.

"You even forgot to pack your bags, I can see."

"You're damn right!"

"With all the money you're making it's not even worth to wear the same clothes twice," I said.

"This is important."

"Any death threats?" I asked with my eyes wide open.

"Don't be silly," she replied. "I've made some contacts in London."

"Don't tell me that the Queen asked you to move to Buckingham palace and set up shop there?"

"Would you please stop it?"

"OK, sorry."

Her face was now two inches away from my nose, "Giallo," she murmured.

"What's Giallo?"

"Aren't you Italian?"
"Yellow."
"What else?"
"Let me think. . . Giallo, the suspense and crime fiction genre popular in Italy in the seventies?"
"Right!"
"What about it?"
"The Giallo team."
"Are we going to slain somebody?"
"No. We're going to make tons of money."

Chapter 10

"...o...okay, good." Grim walked over to Wilfrid, fitted him with a look, and said, "You think so too?"
"Yeah, I think we have the front row seats now."
"Are we going to chat for an hour?"
"Sure. How about a drink?"
"90 minutes."
"1 am."
"Where are we going?"
"Uptown club."
"How about rap?"
"I don't play that game very well."
"Houston, we have an early start. Let's go."

The club was rocking and filled with life, some watching the action on television, while others were milling around drinking sudsy iced rum iced soft drinks in the fancy cups. One hipster wearing a Yankees jersey was complaining about how corporate America was stingy with the ICOs and he couldn't wait to put his lucky number on the usual mailing list. The sitting victim of his sarcasm was Jackpot10, the world-famous bitcoin dealer from China.

Alfonso Borello

Still standing in the hot tub, staring at the refreshing Miami Florida Killa, Jackpot10 smiled and said, "How can you be so hard on yourself?"

Jackpot10 had Murray hooked.

Sure, you should try it, Igor asked, tossing Dice on the dusty patch of earth. Earlier, Mikita had explained how helpful it was to get into competitions, team up, and win such sweet prizes as bright uniforms, sponsored drinks, including free travel, etc. So far, this competition had gone well, apart from one huge freak storm that affected the bracket system. Nick had chosen to stay home and watch the video stream of the action on his phone, as he was the only one enrolled in the chat room. Naturally, he spent his time fixing his worn-out computer keyboard, while nursing a quick cup of tea. About an hour later, however, it struck midnight and all hell broke loose on the block. Astonished by the media frenzy, curiosity piqued, pride stung and quickly ran dry. Had Buchanan's invisible hand somehow imparted some nerve? Have his balls finally hit the ground? Whatever. The host of the chat room, known to everyone as Mexi, was waiting for just such an epiphany. 3700 words later, I typed profit-taking, and the look on his face was priceless.

Guys. Fuck the market makers. Fuck 'em all.

Using Microsoft Azure, I created an alias and began the complex Arabian gambling scam.

Waiting for one of the receiving parties to arrive at my beacon, or rather the Mega code for Gyakuten Saiban IV, I used the rudimentary anti-gin room to enter the victim's origin, alter, and direct deposit the associated coins. I then used a display to hone in on the USB debugging symbols, and assign them reversed numerical codes. Within seconds, all hell broke loose!

Started from Java console, twitter client, opening the native application on Android phone or desktop. Experience has taught me that engineers work better when they are distracted by cocktails and Twine, rather than the latest computer application, coding hell. Flor de Lis, a popular French drink of the moment, apparently offers some stress relief when it comes to troubleshooting. Gianni Moriscu, excellent name among engineers, struck gold in with the contract coding: serial 0558 had three gambling chips and 111,200, the Jackpot. A taxidermy figurine named Breaking Bad dressed as AMC's "Wall St." pulled a trap and urinated on Genji's grave. I received the composite as a separate donation from Thiru Kosalavela, NBC's religious televangelist whose competitors include South Park's, Trey Parker.

△ △ △

Frankfurt am Main, Germany.
DB headquarters.
Kilman was staring at Bloomberg's ECN; he adjusted his hairpiece and stared at the monitor.
"What the hell is going on? Is everybody on vacation?" He gestured to Kaiser who was sitting ten feet away busy tying his atrocious cravat, a second time.
"What's up?" He asked.
"Look at the monitor."
"Not much going on, I can tell."
"I might have to cancel those counter orders."
"It just hit the 180-day high!"

"Right, and I was expecting the cockroaches to load the gun and push it higher."

"All I see is very few trades, no volume at all," Kilman noticed.

"They're probably mourning."

"I'm not sure about that. Definitely, I'm not the one who is going to push it up to new highs."

"Cancel the orders, dammit!"

"I'm about to, but it's a lot of orders, all at different prices."

"Just hit cancel all."

"We can't do that anymore, it's the freakin' new fraud feature which the programmers installed last week."

"Why did they do that?"

"FIFO first in, first out, it's a new rule that came from the trading commission to avoid rogue trading."

"It's going to take several hours to close all these orders."

"How many you have opened?"

"I set it on auto early this morning and the system opened 700 trades."

"You're kidding me!"

"I was expecting some serious heat from those guys."

"All right, let's get to work."

"Wait a minute."

"What?"

"Look at the CNY chart!"

"What about it?"

"The Chinese Yuan."

"Let's load the ECN."

"Dammit, look at the damn volume!"

"It's dropping like a rock."

"Could it be possible that—" Kaiser paused.

T BANDITS

"They switched side."
"Make the call, now!"

Alfonso Borello

Chapter 11

"I drank too much; smoked too many hookahs," Chattanoogan made sure to remind one another.

Grandma greeted the Dutch with a rich Hot McDonald's breakfast; King Chuckwurst and Swissppers; a mug of coffee with orange juice; and the Roll 20/20 at his elbow, which he incessantly manipulated with his index and middle fingers. She passed the aughts Michael Lewis book to him; he grabbed it out of the air and read, in flawless Braille, a passage explaining the various variables of the Dow Jones industrial average.

"What about Sweden?" She asked.

He reread the passage several times, his blue-slip inflatable leg throbbing as he repeated the last paragraph.

"They took a beating."

She looked up to see Mercantilis Leghorn sitting next to her, wearing a dark suit and a white shirt that didn't roll up as low as he liked.

"What's up with them, the bankers?" He asked.

She shook her head, "I called the sets their number and they went away."

"What else?"

She looked up to see DT "You're a fool, IDIOT! Fuck you!" walking towards him.

Glancing back, she saw that Hicks was still sitting on the Punto Swinger; he kept his gaze on the TV, without saying a word.

"They just burned through all their money, that fucking Apple by the way."

"They will never last. Cards on a bank with sovereigns battling it out for market share."

I received an email these days with a digest of incredible bondage-corsets stories: sticky Bob's walkie. I called Fox News and they blocked me.

I impact their chastity? Hookah breaks their back?' I thought feminism was all about equality, campaign cards, shills, find out who your street dealers are! ...was it?' the actress reflexively grimaced. Brezhnev raised an eyebrow.

Sergei shook his head and lit up a cigarette.

"What about it?" he asked.

"The Raja guys," the owner of the red dress replied.

Daisy narrowed her eyes. "...They want us to dig up the stash house," she said. "Who is going to drag their Grillskin of Clam china way back to London?"

The sandwich shop owner shook his head and lit another cigarette.

Muscat tried his best to imitate the French accent, but it was much too thick. Overall, Chinese food tastes better with pepper, of course.

"What are they calling their shrimp fried rice balls?' Grill shouted.

"Hot pepper Babylonian sitcom, I might add," replied Quant.

"Hotels in Shanghai now serve 2 for 500RMB; I stayed at the Five and Dime a few nights ago, the rooms were fucking amazing, must-try; maybe the next time I visit my hostel manager will hire me a cab," Dead Scratch said as he fished his keypad phone out from his sleeve. Click.

"Hot damn," Cohn called.

"Hot damn! Commissar, you've made my day."

Cohn shook his head and lit up a cigarette.

"Have a seat," drinking as much as he could.

Two broke young women entered the room, worked the Jackson Pop super-seller a hole, and stifled a sigh.

"Well, that was a head-scratcher really bad guy," Falisah said.

"They call him the Pumpkin Prince," Morrison replied; he always has a laugh on his face. The Latinas adjusted the color of their, dammit, it's brown! robes.

"How did you find out?" Joanette Williams asked.

"Some internet sleuths, I believe; I only linked to a few articles though."

"Filthy rich suckers, hanging on to every last drop of the South East Asian oil they can, sucking the life out of it."

△ △ △

Singapore – Five weeks later.

Business Times: GIALLO: CHINA'S SECRET WEAPON.

There was a subhead too: How to keep the currency under a tiny bowl of rice and infuriate the west.

As soon as I read the thread on the Oanda news feeder, I hit the chat room.

"Urgent!" I typed.

The green dot blinked several times.
"Go ahead!" Typed Goldmine.
"Read the news feed?"
"Yeah, how did they find out?"
"I have no idea."
"Giallo was never mentioned in the chat room, ever."
"Unless Soraya decided to do a press conference."
"She hasn't been trading in the last couple of days," typed Pipette.
"I haven't seen her either," typed Monstermind.
"I just searched Giallo, and it's all over the places," typed Pipette.
"Give me a second," I replied.
"See nothing here, I just Google it," typed Sumi.
"I searched it in Chinese unless you just became a polyglot," replied Pipette.
"Yeah, right."
"What are they saying?" I asked.
"That we are the movers and shakers."
"I don't get it."
"I just Google it in Chinese, I used Google translate and don't see a thing," typed Pip-A-Lot.
"You're not going to find anything on Google China, dammit!" Replied Pipette.
"Why?"
"They filter words, and censor what they have to."
"So, how do you find things? Do you work for them?"
"Moron! I use a VPN."
"Freakin' cool!"
"So, what else?" I typed.
"A video interview on some financial channel."
"Who's on the damn video?"

"You can only see the interviewer, and hear a woman's voice, sort of modified in pitch."

"What about it?"

"The team Giallo is the best thing that ever happened to China, you can hear from the woman"

"Go ahead." I was freakin' out.

"She's being asked if there's any government involvement."

"What did she say?"

"There's a commercial on right now."

"Can you forward the fuckin' video?"

"It's buffering."

"Hmm. . ."

"All right, now they're talking about Kim Jong-un's mistress and the 'happy endings'"

"Dammit, you're kidding me!"

"Wait, no she said no."

"No what?"

"Nothing, she was never approached by the government."

"So, where is she now?"

T BANDITS

Chapter 12

Tuesday-ish *drinks at the pool* General attendance: 800-1,200 Experts at the game are sitting on one bank and the Potaminians on the other; ghoulish facial expressions include fear and awe. Guillermo del Toro feverishly anticipates the foul ball. Fisheries expert 1/2 block away grimaces as he observes the destruction left by the sucker. Older monk sweats as he observes the mesmerized Monk practice his underhand; the sensor on his webcam twitches a thousand times. Emerging the sorcerer's olla podrampa tea drinks attention as if it's personal. Dead monk got the deadline by offering his frog. Coffee after work: eggs scrambled white and blue; king orange rush; cappuccino. Chickenedîmus scone: spectacular.

After breakfast I hit the local shopping mall for my first shoot; shopping was extra like living in Hong Kong because everything is branded with the names of the companies that make it. Chi-town chic-set on fire by the south wind. Shopping sprawls were avoided at all costs. Subway... no more pedestrians. Citigroup couldn't resist the lure of the switch (to fight the good fight against fraud—the government decided to crackdown). Millions of dollars were bequeathed by the king to victims and various ways to purchase their silence. No dice. Life for Joe was hard despite the reforms that began by Papa Francis. To shed light on the competitive healing environments that the comfort girls fished for clients, I thought I'd settle for a massage.

△ △ △

Sin Bin 19
ECB headquarters.
Brick headquarters. J.P. Morgan has declared war on the Greek government and is pressuring its banks to dump their euros and give them the J.P.M.'s and FFX's of the Wild West.

"Hey, look at the chipping!" Jacques wondered as he tapped on the intercom.

"What are they talking about?" Thomas asked.

"The Swaps' Basement Trader Investigators."

"How did they get our number?"

"We ratted them out."

"What else?"

"Some fishy A.I. went to work."

"Send the hackers a treasure map, and they'll come back with the juicy details."

"Look for Jefferson Nelson, the uh, General of the South, who's usually the nicest guy around."

"He's getting pretty jaded lately."

"The markets are crazy right now. Looks like the only players left are the bitter old' G8 guild."

"Guild?"

"Yeah. Didn't fancy the food either. Out in the cold."

"Fitna killed a few clever kids."
"Shit!"
"Relax; I just got a tip from a Tata associate."
"Who?"
"He's the drag queen of hedge funds. Got the fat monkeys moving with her catchphrases."

P.S. There's a new victim; the Rajan brothers of IP Gold.

Democrat juggernaut claimed into legal cow's den credit gang known as Equícula, where got ripped to shreds by petty legal scam artists – Irish masters– Fed up and madder than hell. They kept blowing heat.

Just last week they slapped 63% tariff at these Portuguese diriks for their crappy footballers. Monster rising. Basket Case wallet burning dim. Starbucks with employees hunkering under the hot pad on a 48-hour strike. Goldman inter alia caught in densest smoke, volume one dominating account. Pressure reduced; decks lowered. Stock market back in the groove. Business as usual at the Equitable Stock Exchange. Concern over Europe hanging by a thread; all banks busted for rogue trading; everyone happy 3 p.m.; tailgate where so many came to drink ale and whore their face; blowholes belted with fire; hundreds jostling for taste; dying swigging, hard. Celebration corner grouchy as a hurricane; people emerging covered head to toe in paint.

Three weeks later I received an email for an interview from a reporter from Forex magazine. I've never heard of such publication before, but I ran a search and found out that it existed and was published every two months. Of course, I never bothered to answer. Three days later I received another Email, again I ignored it. A week later there was a knock on the door. Did I answer? Heck no!

Someone knocked again. I was furious.

Who the hell is knocking on my door?

One of the things that I've always been good at, not by choice, was to ignore people. And today was another fait accompli; perhaps.

After my shower, which was quite long, I went to check the door.

Perhaps they left a note on the door, I thought.

I was right. The note read: WILL BE BACK IN THIRTY, I'M THE REPORTER FROM FOREX MAG.

Well, guess what? The sucker, actually two, did come back.

"Do you mind if we come in?" The one with the Oakley shades asked.

"I do," I answered.

"Well, shall we come back another time?"

"Who are you?" I asked irritated.

"I work for the magazine, I just need twenty minutes," the one with the Oakley said; the one next to him was red as pepper, and scratched his nose.

"Have a sit on the porch; I'll be out in a sec."

I went back in, made some tea, and made them wait twenty minutes; I peeked through the jalousie, they weren't going to give up.

"So, what's up with this damn article you want to write about," I started. The coffee mug was still in my hand, it had and FBI emblem on it. Fake, probably.

They both stared at the mug.

"Do you mind if I use my recorder?" The one with the shades asked.

"If you look to your right, and smile at my camera, I can give you the tape at the end of this, so-called interview," I said with a grin.

The other man with the glabrous skull snorted as he looked up to the right.

"I guess my memory will better be good from now on," Oakley replied.

"What do you want to know?" I asked.

"How's trading?"

"Up and down."

"Do you use an automated system?"

"I don't."

"Do you make use of chat rooms?"

"I just follow some, the ones that play elevator music."

"Is that the kind of music you like?"

"I'm a boring person. I no longer used the Internet. I used PayPal only."

"I see, it makes sense."

"What kind of music you like?" I asked.

"Not much time to listen to music nowadays, not for me."

"How about police talks?"

He scratched his head, and finally removed his Oakley.

"Relax; I'm just here to gather some information."

"You're pretty bad as a reporter; as a martinet for the National Futures Association or whatever, you're also a disaster; you may want to practice a little bit more on your body language. You guys just started?"

They weren't amused.

"OK, let's make it short."

"Right," I replied.

"You've been giving financial advice without a license, according to our findings."

"Are you accusing me of wrongdoing?"

"You might want to stop doing those chat, technically speaking, it's like giving financial advice."

"You're beating the wrong drum!"

"I'm telling you, just friendly, stop doing that crap."

"If you have anything to charge me with, go ahead."

"Don't be a fool."

"Go ahead!"

"Listen, I'm here with you, and tell you what I told you; just doing my job."

"Go back to the office, and tell your DA to press charges. If he doesn't have anything, to begin with, just tell him to leave me alone."

"There's no need for DAs here," said the one with the red face.

"You know what the problem is?"

They both stood up.

"Go after those damn rating agencies, regulate them! Stop blaming the traders and everything else. Traders go after the trend and always will. You've got a bunch of, so-called experts who foment nothing but panic. Who do they work for? Who the hell they work for? For an audience? For the banks to jack up the interest rates?"

"Countries have been borrowing nothing more than they did in the last thirty years. But of course, now, because of the agencies, because of the panic, because of all these rogue institutions which crave to get fatter and fatter, they have to pay a whopping seven percent interest, to keep up with an aging population, who never bothered with video games and other crap."

They were still listening, Oakley gazed at the camera.

"Leave us alone, would you? Go after the real troublemakers. And stop reading The Economist, they are Eurosceptics."

Chapter 13

"We wrote panicked checks," complains Bornhiu. "And now they kick Uncle Ninja in the Samba and FOCUS RIGHT BACK on Loafers and The Rocks!"

By Googling "illegal tender," one is led to media sites that report only what-the-hell-the-organization-wants. Stock exchange info is scant either way.

Nick Karpeles, the mastermind of the ever-memorable wallet the grizzled cookie at the head of energy trading room, extolled the favor; 350 bitcoins is chump change by global standards, but bragging rights are right around the corner. Consortium fever is high.

Currency in a pinch? Need I remind you? Ka-Ching!

Business as usual at the White House? Won't happen. Scarce resources. Horses ahead. Already speaking to Xi Jinping. Talking currency.

Cyprus talks dead. Nothing to see here. Cycle back to the Goddess.

Officials from the European Central Bank monitored the conference call and pushed a button that triggered an exchange rate increase. Kraken, the Chinese financial center, registered the event.

The U.S. dollar was up about 2%, pushing the Euro one paltry pennant. Sell order at the 193 per dollar low was fulfilled. U.S. Treasuries fell by 1.5%. Gold climbed another $1, signaling more strength to come. Here comes the chancellor!

Michaël Walli (always high after 5:03 PM), governor of the European Central Bank, was on the line. Everyone in the office lights fainted. Opioid effect. Wu Jie, chairman of the J Club fashion house, triggered an electromechanical wrist spiking alarm. The lights went out in the research room.

Wu studied his e-mail account for ten minutes. He sighed and roused himself with a brisk jog.

Fortune favors the adventurous here at the Atlanta Financial Center. After analyzing newly published research on commodity trading bots, dummy companies, stolen sensor data, and steganography, we calculated that the only way to make a quick buck was by being the first to break the 'transparisteau' security. So now we are bussing bullets. Ready, set?

△ △ △

"Aha! familiar faces here! ♪ " Weiss joked.

"Hey guys, was the e-news looking good?"

"Nope. Not much traffic, obviously. Stink up, perverts."

"You're right. Sad."

They stared at the ceiling. It was pitchforks and torches time. Mt. Gox was getting ready to hit the jackpot, folks. China will pay for LosersClub with gold.

Worry not, traders! China will never give in to economic weakness and barbwire will not deter them. Trump OD on Propecia, tweets like a madman and spits rubber bullets; can't negotiate a shit. Long live Scaramucci.

△ △ △

X-Trading Room
GBP>USD
High: TBD or more, set your auto limit to "Too High." A trader's number is his window of opportunity to exploit weak links in the trading network. Trade your way to the top. A reminder: there's a new victim in town (Hong Kong): active duty military. Gas mask? (with VAT tax increase) Check. Combat boots? Check. Money talks.

"Hey, look at that chart! Dynamite Empire in 2 days. All metrics above 600,000 won. Yuan limit 7,500,000, up, activate Greece and takes full advantage of the elite naysayers. Quick, please!"

ICYMI—"Good Morning, Everyone. Happy New Year!" :o)

P.S. For those who aren't familiar with the Greek system, it's a unique breed of accounting known as the Greek for the street. Essentially, a volunteer rolls the dice and bets big. The better he slaps on the hook, the higher the squats. For example, if Bill Gates bet a billion dollars on the scorecard, then Hell, sure, he whistles.

Speaking of China, they're going to have an economic bonanza just like before. Yuan will be trading way above par. It's going to take years. And it's going to be REALLY, REALLY expensive. Ever wonder how Warren Buffett pulls his punches?

Fast forward...

The Giallo team attracted more than 150,000 new traders

(20+ bankers, 7+ former stockbrokers, 3 investment bankers, legal advisers, CPAs, Buddhist monks, sports scientists, social/sex workers, etc.) in the months that follow, and was going strong. Stock day traders converted to Forex trading, and Forex traders converted to the currency which knew only one direction. Money was flowing better than anyone could have imagined; it wasn't like playing blackjack at a casino, with the fear of being spotted by the eyes in the sky; this was a better deal, a better game, a solid cash cow, with no backrooms.

There were days when the chat room wasn't even active; everybody knew what to do. What? Push the Yuan lower and lower. No more indicators, no more resistance; keep placing sell orders, market orders, limit orders, sell limit, whatever, as long as the cardinal direction was south. In the end, even ass bandit Billy O'Reilly could have become a currency trader; no, it wasn't a joke anymore.

China is finally a happy nation. Remember when in the seventies they were all riding a bicycle and wore uniforms?

Now they're shopping for Mercedes, BMWs, Ferraris, Prada, and Gucci; why not? Michelangelo Antonioni was the only filmmaker from the west invited to make a documentary, which of course ended up being an Italian disastro, a mockumentary, according to Chinese political insiders.

Now they have the last laugh; cheap currency, cheap labor, cheap everything. Quality isn't bad if Apple and other western powerhouses dictate the manufacturing process; the rest is subject to interpretation.

What about us, the Giallo team?

We did our part. Unfortunately, nothing (at that pace) lasts forever. The banks couldn't knock us down, the governments couldn't either; no matter how much the G20 hated us. They used every threat in the book. Headlines after headlines, IRS audits that never materialized, government rats monitoring our chats, but too stupid to trade, an olla podrida of trumped-up charges of sexual assaults a la Julian Assange, and regulations which became subject of mockery from country to country. The rules were, of course, written by attorneys, poetasters, and dictated by bureaucrats; but in the end, they never understood each other, and everything was lost in translation. A new rule conflicted with the others, and it kept going and going.

Are we still trading? Don't know, don't ask.

Alfonso Borello

Sci-Fi

Sample Chapter

Also, by Alfonso Borello

The spaceship was overbooked, some had to sit on the floor for dust. There were all kinds of people, including refugees. I didn't see any flight attendant, not that I was expecting one, considering the price, but it would have been nice to have one, just to see the emergency procedures in case of trouble.

Nobody looked at each other. Strange that so few people behaved this differently. We were heading away from earth and for good.

Suddenly, one of the passengers came out of his shadow and broke the silence, "what time are we supposed to arrive on Mars?"

He looked straight at me, a little uncomfortable. No one bothered to answer, few glanced at their watch.

"What do you wanna do on Mars?" I asked. He shook his head, then stared at his feet.

"It is hard to say, but I do plan to do some experimenting there and have the opportunity to try to improve the surroundings."

"You might need a crew." A lady said, with an almost happy grin.

"You could do it?" I asked.

"Sure, if I could find enough supplies." He smiled.

The same lady was listening closely. She looked at him with a blend of curiosity and surprise and tried to smile.

"And you, young lady, why are you running away from Earth?" I asked.

She frowned, "I'm moving to Mars because I have to, to save my race. I didn't like the life I was having on Earth. You can save your race if only you know what you want. The Martians are ideal creatures, only slightly above the 'surface' on life, in spite of our technical superiority. We can improve our conditions for life on Mars, but it will take time. When Abraham spoke to God, he didn't say to 'make war' or to 'make peace'. He said 'Let be strife in the heavens'. This 'peace' the earth men want isn't any peace at all. They want war. Why? Because all this 'peace' that they're talking about is so pointless. It's just a shame—a way of getting money for more money. They want wars, and the only thing that could justify it is more money. Some are against our love, our understanding, even our truth."

"They're really against anything," said Wendy, the tall girl with the long brown hair standing next to me. She seemed to speak from the inside. "This isn't about politics, it's about us."

Henderson, the developer-wanna-be moved forward confidently. "All right, then. I'm going to tell you about the Martians. How they live, why they don't live like civilized people, and what they would do if they could."

"Wait a minute," said Austin, a short stocky dude next to one of the emergency exit. Thoughtful. "Hope we won't have to swim in the Martian lava."

"Let's land the ship first, then we'll see," said Henderson.

Austin held in hands out, looking apprehensively. "I can't understand it." There was no sound. Suddenly a blast from the side, in the distance. Most likely from the other side of the ship. A tall man nicked named the professor, because of his look, was standing by a small door, probably airlocked, he said something but his voice trailed off. His eyes bulging. His head tipped forward.

"Let's get out of here," he said.

Wendy and Betsy, the girl that was next to me before, leaped to their feet and stood in front of the tall man in a panic, "What's the matter, professor?" The airlock door clanged open and he disappeared through it. They looked after him as he vanished. I watched for a second, then I heard a small bang.

"Dead?" I asked.

"Dead," said Betsy.

"Why?" Asked Henderson.

"What happened?" Asked Austin.

"Professor is dead," said Wendy. "He forced the door open and he was thrown outside."

"How about the airlock door?" I asked.

"Servo auto-lock," said Henderson. "For safety."

"Call it magic," I said.

The girls' eyes narrowed. "What about that horrible sound?" Betsy asked.

"Probably an asteroid or a black-hole," explained Henderson.

"Is the airlock sealed?" I asked.

'The force door is sealed, and the airlock is sealed," double-checked Henderson. " We're safe. "

"I hope Mars is a big place, with lots of little towns and stuff. I can't wait to get there, weeks in these cramped quarters will drive me crazy after a while," said Wendy.

"Well, lots of ambitious folks on the ship, we have to be cautious, I don't want to see another one of us doing a Peter Pan kind of exaltation," I said.

Austin was getting bored and dialed his cell; we all looked at each other, "maybe he has an interplanetary plan," said Betsy with a wondering look.

"I moved to Mars," shouted Austin, gesturing with his hand to the map. "Do you mean the moon is outside?"

"The moon is full of water, isn't it?" Asked Betsy.

"Yes," said Henderson.

"But it's all ice," said Austin.

"All water?" Asked Betsy, again.

There was a smirk in Henderson's mouth.

"There's nothing there that would be water, is there?" Asked Wendy.

Henderson shrugged.

△ △ △

"Maybe we're going to Venus!" exclaimed Betsy.

"What, you want Venus too?" asked Austin.

" If we go there, we have to be careful, it's not that safe," replied Henderson. " It's not as stable as Mars."

" Well, then, let's keep it that way," said Betsy.

An hour later, almost everyone fell asleep except for me and Henderson, who just sat up and looked around.
" What's wrong, is everything OK?" I asked.
" I think we've missed our stop," Henderson said, staring at his watch. " It's almost 9:30."
I looked around the room.
"Maybe the professor who played Peter Pan had a plan," I said.
"Maybe he was drunk, he was thinking of robotic tones. Who knows, he'll be fine wherever he is now." "I think we're going to have to do something, or we're never going to get out of here."
"The crew never came out to check on us," I said.
"There's no crew," said Henderson.
Austin was awake a looked out the window, "I feel like I haven't talked to anyone for a while. I don't know, maybe I was too focused on my Earth life, I'm a little out of touch with things here. I need to get off this ship and come back refreshed," said Austin."
"Some of you had grown tired of his obsession with Earth. Maybe it was all selfishness, maybe you just miss Earth," said Henderson.
"What about the people back home, do they miss us?" Asked Austin.
I smiled a little, "Not as much as you think, the majority of them don't know much about us, not even of our mission" I said.
"If we at least could watch TV, nothing fancy, even Martian news," said Betsy while brushing her hair with a travel-size toothbrush.

"On the other wing, they're all drinking coffee and talking about how it's getting colder and colder and they want to take some pictures of the moon," said Austin. "It's like this place is not a ship anymore, but an alien environment, like living in a frozen space capsule."

"Really?" said Henderson.

There was clattering in the hallway, Wendy glanced out the window. Austin took a quick look outside. There was a strange green light coming from the sky, it seemed to be moving rapidly around. A figure from the spaceship was emerging from the other window and moving down through like from some time warp.

The room was quiet except the sounds of the landing, Austin turned the lights off and stood quietly next to Wendy and looked around.

"That's creepy as shit, but we're finally landing on Martian Paradise," said Austin, staring a little longer in silent contemplation, as the craft approached and stopped.

Thirty days on Mars looks different every minute: The landscape looks beautiful from every angle, with deep grooves carved in every cliff along the Martian coastline, almost a Riviera Ligure, less dramatic in character, but more impressive considering it took hundreds to construct, almost every inch seemed carefully thought to preserve as a habitat for future colonists.

Austin was a good coder, and Henderson brought a lot of useful plans, and I was trying to get myself into an exploratory phase, it may have just happened that we met under some circumstances that produced a positive signal.

After some drift and a lot of recuperation, I started working on Mars Life Support, to ensure that all the food and water that we get from the vicinity of the planet Mars and particularly the solar system at large is safe for us. The higher-level thinking about the real values of Mars life made me fascinated by the long ways that we push into the unknown.

If the human species follows the predicted evolutionary path, we are going to get tired, we are going to lose interest, we are going to want the next. And so on. We're not going to arrive at a direct link to the stars, a path that gets us there eventually. It may have, in the past, been possible to get there soon, but our bodies and brains have gone through a series of evolutionary stages that have taught us to live that way, to make life pay, and to refuse to stay within the known boundaries.

Again, this provides us with an opportunity to break the rules. Mars is a territory whose perimeter we cannot pass by, there are many lessons to be learned. I began working on a new way to think about planning for Mars to help in the solving of the challenges we are facing: data. If we do things effectively, we can use the information that we accumulate on the way around to analyze it in new ways, so that we can come up with better methods and techniques for serving Mars.

www.ingramcontent.com/pod-product-compliance
Lightning Source LLC
Chambersburg PA
CBHW020607220526
45463CB00006B/2493